Part One

Frederick Noad
First Book for the Guitar

GUITAR

Illustrations by Charles Boyer

G. SCHIRMER, Inc.

DISTRIBUTED BY

HAL•LEONARD®
CORPORATION
7777 W. BLUEMOUND RD. P.O. BOX 13819 MILWAUKEE, WI 53213

About The Author

Frederick Noad, the author of a number of widely used educational guitar books and anthologies, was born in Belgium. Educated in England, he is a graduate of Oxford University.

Originally trained in the violin and piano, Noad took up the guitar in his early teens, and was later a performing member in master classes of Andres Segovia and Julian Bream.

After coming to the United States in 1957 he founded the "Spanish Guitar Center" in Hollywood, modeled on a similar teaching establishment in London, which he directed until 1965. During this period he studied composition with Mario Castelnuovo-Tedesco at the latter's home in Beverly Hills.

In 1966 Noad launched the series "Playing the Guitar" for educational television. The programs were enthusiastically received from coast to coast, and are credited with introducing 100,000 new players to the instrument.

Noad has been a faculty member of the University of California, Irvine, and the California Institute of the Arts. He performs as a soloist, as part of a duet team, in concert with a lyric tenor and also as a continuo player in early opera. In addition to the guitar he plays the lute and theorbo.

CONTENTS

TO THE READER

This book makes three assumptions. The first is that you have just acquired a guitar and are ready for the pleasure and challenge of beginning to play. The second is that you know absolutely nothing about music or how it is written. The third is that you know nothing about the guitar itself.

Obviously if you *do* know something already you have an advantage, and this will help you through the early stages: But even so it will be a good idea to go carefully through the checklists provided to be absolutely sure that you have not missed some fundamental point.

For best results with this method, the secret is to go one step at a time, not trying to do too much at one sitting, and particularly not trying to jump ahead to the more difficult material.

Progression by simple stages is the key to major achievement. There is a saying in the East that a journey of a thousand miles begins with a single step; and the designers of do-it-yourself kits, from ham radios to harpsichords, have found that a person of average ability can construct amazingly complex finished items by following a clear progression of instructions. However, just as the omission of one part from an electronic kit can mean disaster, so in learning music the skipping of steps can mean failure to form the groundwork on which future progress depends.

This book is a practical manual; so as information is given, there is an action required to reinforce the memory. If the action involves saying something out loud, for instance when counting, do it without feeling foolish. As with names, verbal repetition is a strong aid to memorization.

If you possibly can, go to a teacher. Many of the musical exercises are designed for the teacher to play with the student, and they sound fuller and more interesting played this way. Also, your overall progress will be speeded up by the help that a good teacher can give you. But if access to a teacher is impossible, you can still achieve wonders if you remember that you must be the teacher as well as the student and impose on yourself a systematic and self-critical approach.

The main purpose is enjoyment. With the right start you can look forward to many years of pleasure and satisfaction. Learning to read music is not nearly as difficult as most people think, and with the correct approach it is well within the capabilities of the average seven year old child. The music symbols are not academic dogma; they are a tool for you to use to achieve your goals. You are the master, and they represent the servant that assists you on your musical journey.

The physical movements involved in playing music are known as "technique." Some beginning books leave this to the teacher and concentrate on musical notation only. This book attempts to give you the clearest possible explanation of how to perform the important basic movements in case a teacher is not available. Habits must be formed for the movements to become automatic, and it is as easy to form good habits as bad ones. But bad habits are hard to lose, so particular care in the first stages will save much time in the future.

Good luck, and welcome to the world of the guitar.

NOTE TO THE TEACHER

As far as possible I have tried to make this first approach to the guitar an enjoyable experience for both student and teacher. The exercises are in the form of duets, so that even the most basic process of note-learning can be fun. This usually comes as a surprise to the student who does not expect to be participating in "real music" at such an early stage, and his delight in his achievement serves as an incentive to both parties.

The scope of Part One has been carefully defined to include a fully illustrated description of all major techniques, the complete notes of the first position including accidentals, and the fundamentals of music up to the eighth note. The more advanced subjects, such as the dotted quarter note, theory of keys and scales, and notes faster than the eighth note, have been reserved for Part Two. Part Three completes the basic knowledge appropriate to the first year of study.

ABOUT THE GUITAR

This book is about the nylon-strung guitar of the type shown in the illustration. It is known variously as the classical (or classic) guitar, the concert guitar, or the finger-style guitar to distinguish it from other types with steel strings which are sometimes amplified electrically.

The classical guitar needs no amplification since of all the types it has the greatest natural resonance, and when professionally played can be clearly heard in a full-sized auditorium.

The same musical notation is shared by all forms of the instrument, but electric guitars are usually played with a plectrum of plastic or tortoise shell whereas the nylon-strung guitar is played with the fingers (or fingernails as we shall shortly see).

NAMING THE PARTS

For future reference it is important to know the correct name for the various parts of the guitar. After studying the diagram (Fig. 1), identify each of the following on your own instrument.

Fig. 1 THE ANATOMY OF THE CLASSICAL GUITAR.

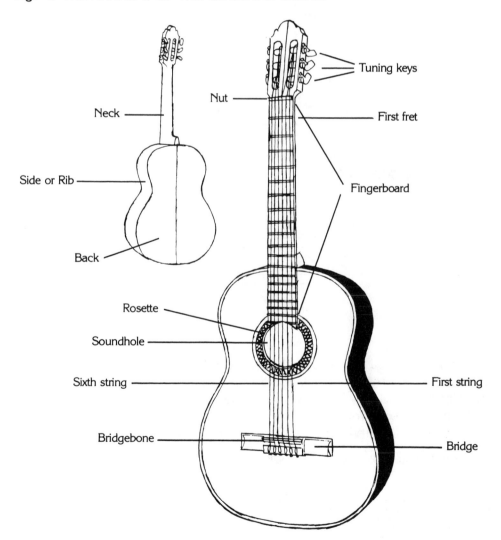

Of particular importance is the numbering of the strings. Remember that the first string is the thinnest, highest in pitch, and closest to the floor when you are sitting in the normal playing position.

HOW GUITAR MUSIC IS WRITTEN

The following section explains all the musical symbols used in this book. The purpose is to give you an overall picture and a general section for reference; however, each item is introduced and practiced in the lessons which follow so as to build up the real familiarity that comes with use.

Music for the guitar is written on what is known as a STAFF, consisting of five horizontal lines. Each line and each space between represents a musical sound, lower sounds at the bottom of the staff and higher at the top.

At the beginning of each staff is a CLEF sign. The sign illustrated is always used for the guitar, and is known as a TREBLE or G CLEF (since it curls around the line that represents the note G). Other instruments of higher or lower pitch use different clefs, which indicate the set of notes more commonly used by that instrument.

The notes represented by the treble clef are as follows:

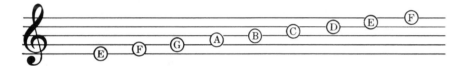

For memorization purposes they are usually divided into two sets:

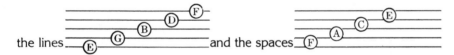

Obviously the nine lines and spaces are not enough for all the notes, so extra lines are drawn above and below the staff where necessary

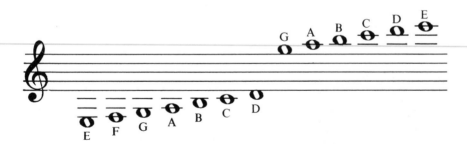

The extra lines are known as ledger lines. Notice that only the letters A to G are used for naming notes; after G the progression starts again with another A. You will soon find out in practice the similiarity between one A and the next one eight notes (an OCTAVE) higher or lower. Your ear will tell you that although one is higher in pitch than the other they have a similiarity in sound.

Now here are the six strings of the guitar expressed in notation.

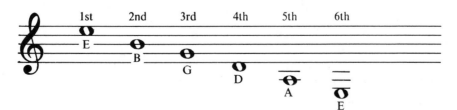

NOTES AND RESTS

The symbols drawn on a line or space indicate how long each note is to last. Periods of silence are known as RESTS, and each note has an equivalent rest sign. Measurement is by even counts, also known as beats from the expression "beating time," which is what a conductor does with his baton.

The table below shows the note lengths in beats when each beat lasts a quarter note (the commonest time you will encounter).

SYMBOL	NAME	EQUIVALENT REST	DURATION
𝅝	Whole Note (Semibreve)	▬	Four Beats
𝅗𝅥·	Dotted Half Note (Dotted Minim)	▬·	Three Beats
𝅗𝅥	Half Note (Minim)	▬	Two Beats
𝅘𝅥	Quarter Note (Crochet)	𝄽	One Beat
𝅘𝅥𝅮	Eighth Note (Quaver)	𝄾	Half a Beat

The names given are those used in the United States. The names in brackets are those in common usage in England.

A dot increases any note by half its value again. Hence a dotted quarter note lasts one and a half beats, as discussed later.

Two or more eighth notes may be joined together thus: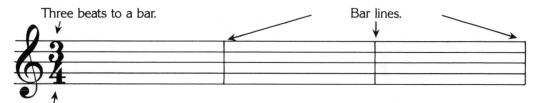

The line joining them is known as a BEAM. The thin upright line is a STEM.

To assist counting and rhythm music is divided into BARS or MEASURES of a given number of counts. Bar lines are drawn vertically as shown below. At the beginning of every piece a TIME SIGNATURE shows how many beats there are in each bar, and also how long each beat lasts. The *upper* number tells you how many beats are in each bar, the *lower* number the duration of each beat.

Three beats to a bar.   Bar lines.

Each beat lasts a quarter note.

Much of the above may seem difficult to grasp in theory, but it will become clear as you start to play from the music. It is necessary to list this rather large number of theoretical points because even the first and easiest piece of music must contain a staff, clef sign, time signature, etc. However, a basic concept will do at this point if you remember that this section is here for reference.

Now here is a checklist to see how many of the points you already remember.

1. Which letters are used for musical notes?

2. Which notes are represented by the lines of the staff? Which by the spaces?

3. How many beats does a half note last? A dotted half note?

4. Why are clef signs used?

5. What is a time signature? Which number indicates how many beats there are in a bar?

6. What are bar lines? Why are they used?

TUNING

Fig. 2 ATTACHING THE STRINGS
TO THE BRIDGE.

Fig. 3 ATTACHING THE STRINGS
TO THE TUNING KEYS.

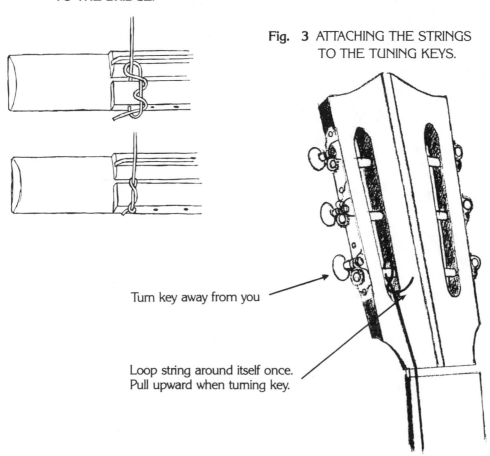

Turn key away from you

Loop string around itself once.
Pull upward when turning key.

With the strings correctly tied as shown above, the easiest way to tune in
the early stages is to align the strings with the same notes on a piano. The
diagram shows which notes to use.

Fig. 4 THE RELATIONSHIP OF GUITAR TUNING TO NOTES ON THE PIANO.

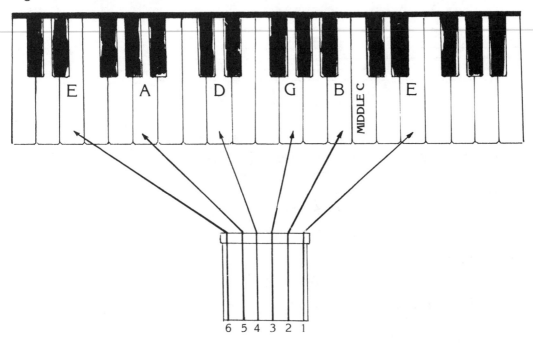

The tuning keys are used to tighten or loosen each string until it sounds the
same as the given note on the piano. At first it is hard to hear if two notes are
exactly in tune, but this comes with practice.

Begin by tuning the strings as closely as possible to the piano, then check them off in the steps given below.

1. Play the 6th string with a left hand finger behind the 5th fret. The note should be the same as the 5th string played open (i.e. with no left hand finger on it). If it is not the same, adjust the 5th string (*not* the 6th).

2. Now play the 5th string at the 5th fret. It should be the same as the 4th string open. If not, adjust the *4th* string.

3. Follow the same steps, playing the 4th string at the 5th fret to obtain the sound for the 3rd string open. Adjust the 3rd string if necessary.

4. Now there is a slight change in procedure. The 3rd string must be played at the *4th* fret (not the 5th) to give the same sound as the 2nd string. Adjust the 2nd string if necessary.

5. Finally play the 2nd string at the 5th fret to obtain the sound for the 1st string.

The above procedure is known as *relative* tuning, each string being tuned in relation to its neighbor. When the relationships are understood and have been practiced a few times, it only becomes necessary to have the pitch for one string, since the others can be tuned to it.

If a piano is not available, all music stores can provide either a pitch pipe or tuning fork to help you establish a correct pitch.

Of the two, the pitch pipe is easier to handle since it can be sounded while held in the mouth thereby leaving both hands free to play and adjust the tuning. A vibrating tuning fork must be held with the handle touching a resonant surface to be properly heard, and this ties up one of the hands. However, the tuning fork has the advantage of greater accuracy.

SPECIAL TUNING TIPS

1. A very small turn of the tuning key may not be sufficient to change the pitch of the string, due to play in the mechanism. A reasonably positive movement must be made.

2. If a string is minutely high in pitch, it may be brought down the necessary fraction by stretching it with the right hand. This is done by taking hold of the string and giving it a twist as if turning a handle.

3. The stretching procedure described above is particularly useful in taking the slack out of new strings. Otherwise new strings have to be constantly tuned since they keep going down when played. Beginners often think that this is because the strings are slipping, but if they are correctly tied as shown in the diagrams no slippage will occur.

If you still have problems after working through the above steps, do not hesitate to seek the help of a musical friend or a music shop. The staff at any shop where guitars are sold is accustomed to helping beginners, and a live demonstration can be most helpful. Now, as a quick check before continuing, answer the following questions.

1. What is an open string?

2. What is relative tuning?

3. Which string must be sounded at the 4th fret to give the pitch for its neighbor above?

4. How may a string be lowered in pitch without using the tuning key?

5. Why do new strings need to be stretched?

BEGINNING TO PLAY

Fig. 5 THE PLAYING POSITION

THE PLAYING POSITION

Study the diagram, and try to take a position as close to it as possible. The following points are important.

1. Sit on the *front* of the chair. The position involves leaning forward slightly, which is more difficult if you sit back in the chair.

2. Be sure to use a footstool or something similar to raise your left leg. This is the main support point for the guitar.

3. Take the weight of your right forearm on the guitar. Don't curl the arm around the guitar, since this will throw the right hand into the wrong position.

4. When you need to look at the front of the guitar, move your head forward rather than tilting the guitar back to you. This way you maintain control and domination of the instrument.

THE RIGHT HAND

Now look at the right hand in the diagram. Notice that the knuckles are aligned with the strings. If you can remember this one point, you will be well on the way to establishing a good right hand position. The wrist should be arched up from the face of the guitar, and should *never* touch it.

THE REST STROKE

Fig. 6 THE REST-STROKE.

B. The detail shows the nail in relation to the string

A. Preparation: Notice the angle of the finger.

C. Completion: The finger comes to rest on the adjacent string.

D. For the strongest sound the nail pulls directly across to the adjacent string.

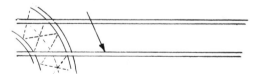

E. For better tone quality the nail travels in the direction shown.

Preparation

Place the tip of the index finger on the first string, so that the fingertip is in contact with it, with the nail projecting over the string. The left-hand edge of the nail (as you look down on your hand) is in contact with the string.

Completion

Draw the finger towards the second string. Your nail first pulls against the original string, then releases it to play the note. The fingertip comes to *rest* on the second string, giving the movement its name; THE REST STROKE.

TONE QUALITY

Anyone can play a *loud* note, but the object is to make a beautiful one. The movement that produces the best tone is quite subtle, although easy to perform when clearly understood. It is described in considerable detail because it is the single most important secret in the development of your individual touch, and is unfortunately ignored or inadequately described in most beginning books.

First consider the following analogy. Imagine that the string is a rope stretched in front of you a foot or so above the ground, and that you are going to make it vibrate by using a spade whose tip is curved in a half-moon shape (representing your nail).

The simplest way to make the rope vibrate would be to put the tip of the spade on the far side of the rope and pull it towards you. The rope would slide down to the extreme tip as you pulled, then would slip clear and be free to vibrate. This represents a note played with a head-on attack, which would produce good volume but a somewhat harsh tone.

For a more pleasing sound let us return to the rope and the spade. First, the handle of the spade would be angled to the left so that it was about 15 degrees away from the vertical (or at ten o'clock if that is easier to imagine). Next, the blade of the spade would be placed on the far side of the rope with the left cutting edge only in contact with it, at a point on the spade where the half-moon taper begins. The right edge would be just clear of the rope, so that the whole blade forms a slight angle away from it.

To produce the subtler vibration, you would draw the spade towards you angling it slightly to your right so that the rope would slide down the left hand cutting edge, be caught by the tip, and finally released. The amount of obstruction offered by the tip could be precisely controlled by the angle of the blade as the movement was performed; the flatter the blade to the rope, the more obstruction.

This essentially is the movement made by the nail when it plays a note, and the main secret of good guitar sound is contained in this basic movement.

Two final important points: First, the movement is made by the finger alone, and does not involve the whole hand. Second, the finger should have a comfortable curve, and this curve should be maintained throughout the stroke. Resist any tendency of the joints to straighten out when pull is applied to the string. In our analogy this would be the equivalent of using a spade with a rubber handle, which would be very hard to control with precision.

THE SHAPE OF THE NAILS

Before beginning your experiments, it is important to have the nail correctly shaped. Obviously if the nail is too long, it is liable to hang up on the string. If it is too short, it cannot give enough impetus to the stroke. Finally, if it is square in shape the corner will catch, making it almost impossible to play. If necessary, adjust the shape before proceeding.

File the nails so that a thin, even ridge may be seen above the fingertip when you look at your hand with the palm facing you. Finally, smooth the nails with fine (600 grade) sandpaper to remove any roughness left from the filing. This last step is essential if a scratchy tone is to be avoided when playing with the nails.

FINGER IDENTIFICATION

It is important to recognize how the fingers of each hand are identified, and this is shown in Fig. 7. The left hand is simple, the fingers being numbered 1-4 with no number for the thumb since it is not used. For the right hand the initial letters are used of the appropriate Spanish words: *Pulgar*=Thumb, *Indicio*=Index finger, *Medio*=Middle finger and *Anular*=Ring finger.

Fig. 7 FINGER IDENTIFICATION.
These indications are universally used and should be memorized.

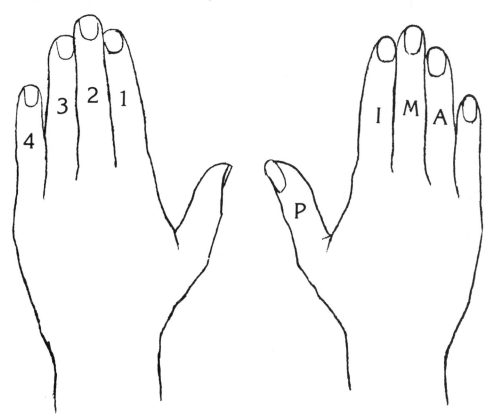

FIRST PRACTICE OF THE REST STROKE. ALTERNATION.

The movements described above should be tried out experimentally on the upper three strings. Try for a good quality note using first the index (*i*), then the middle (*m*) fingers. In playing a series of notes, always alternate the fingers. You may start with *i* or *m*—there is not fixed rule—but avoid using the same finger twice. Alternating the fingers produces a natural rhythm comparable to walking. Repeating the same finger is like hopping when you could walk. As one finger plays, the other should move forward to be ready to play in its turn.

THE LEFT HAND

The basic movements of the left hand are quite simple. The fingers press immediately behind the metal frets, shortening the vibrating length of the string and thereby changing its pitch.

The overall position of the left hand and wrist is of great importance. A good position ensures maximum reach, a minimum of excessive movement, and general stability. Of particular importance is the position of the thumb.

Fig. 8 LEFT-HAND POSITION.

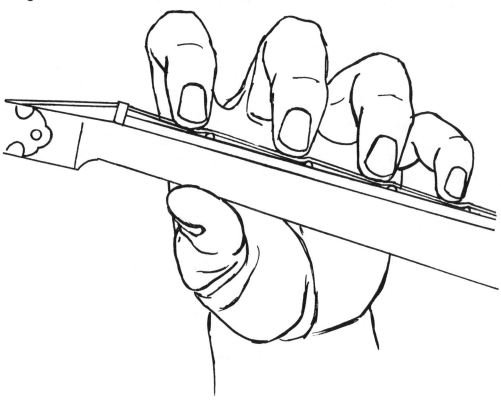

The illustration shows the correct position for the left hand with all fingers in place. The following points are important:

1. The thumb presses against the center of the back of the neck, just forward of the first fret. The pressure is as light as possible consistent with holding the strings down.

2. The first joint of the thumb does not bend. Allowing the joint to bend gives rise to insecurity in the left hand, since the thumb functions as a stable point of reference.

3. The fingers are as vertical as possible in relation to the fingerboard. Adjust the wrist to achieve this.

FIRST LEFT-HAND EXERCISE

The following exercise is excellent for stretching out and strengthening the left hand, and may profitably be practiced every day for the first few weeks.

1. With the thumb in the correct position, hammer down the first finger behind the first fret of the sixth string. Make as loud a sound as possible.
2. Leaving the first finger where it is, hammer in a similar way with the second finger behind the second fret.
3. Repeat the procedure with the third finger. Notice that it is much harder to reach right up to the third fret with the other two fingers in position; but try anyway, because this is an area where stretch must be developed.
4. Complete the movement by hammering with the little finger behind the fourth fret.
5. Repeat all the movements on the fifth and remaining strings. Remember to leave each finger down after it has hammered. On the third, second, and first strings it is harder to make the note sound with the left hand alone, but it *can* be done with practice.

PUTTING BOTH HANDS TOGETHER

The time has now arrived to co-ordinate the two hands in playing a series of notes. The right hand will play alternating rest strokes, and the left hand will move up a fret at a time as in the previous exercise.

1. Place the left hand first finger behind the first fret of the top (first) string. With the right hand play a firm rest stroke with the *i* finger.
2. Leaving the first finger in position, place the second finger behind the second fret. Play a rest stroke with the *m* finger.
3. Leaving the first two fingers down, continue to play the third and fourth frets, doing rest strokes with *i* and *m* in turn.
4. Repeat the procedure on the second and third strings.

FURTHER DEVELOPMENT

When you feel confident with the above exercise try it in reverse, playing from the fourth to the first fret on each of the top three strings. In working backwards it is not necessary to place all the fingers in advance. Simply start with the fourth finger, then the third and so on. As a final development try the following complete exercise.

1. Starting at the sixth string, play upwards from frets one to four, following on with the fifth and all other strings.
2. When you arrive at the highest point, the fourth fret of the first string, start down and play all strings from fourth to first fret. This is an excellent co-ordination exercise which will prepare your hands for playing from music.

THE FREE STROKE

For the sake of completeness we will consider briefly the other principal right hand movement known as the FREE STROKE.

The free stroke is easy to understand, since the movements are similar to those of the rest stroke except in the final phase. Instead of coming to rest, the finger just clears the adjacent string and comes to a halt in the air approximately above it.

Fig. 9 THE FREE STROKE.

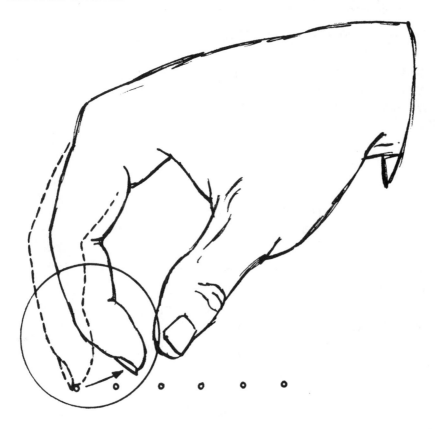

The free stroke becomes important in the performance of chords and arpeggios, which are considered in detail after sufficient notes have been learned. For now, the stroke may be practiced experimentally to distinguish it clearly from the rest stroke.

CONCLUSION

This first section on basic technique is a very important one, since at the end of it you are really playing the guitar. Remember particularly to check the following:

1. Is your sitting position correct, as in the illustration?

2. Is your left arm relaxed?

3. Is your thumb behind the neck? Not bent at the joint?

4. Are your left-hand fingers as vertical as possible when you play?

5. Are your right-hand knuckles on a line with the strings?

6. Is your right wrist correctly arched?

If the exercises have been thoroughly practiced and you can comfortably co-ordinate the two hands, you are now ready for the challenge and enjoyment of beginning to play from music.

NOTES ON THE FIRST STRING

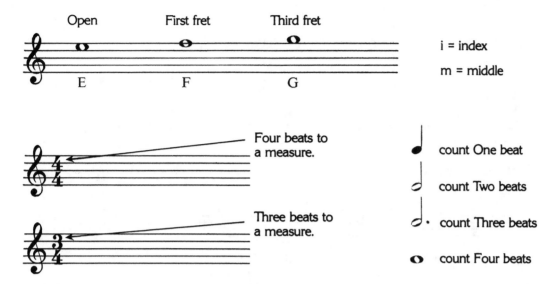

Open	First fret	Third fret
E	F	G

i = index

m = middle

Four beats to a measure.

Three beats to a measure.

♩   count One beat

♩   count Two beats

♩.   count Three beats

𝅝   count Four beats

The diagrams above summarize the information necessary to play the exercises that follow. First memorize the three notes by playing them and saying aloud the letter names of the notes. Use rest strokes as learned in the previous section, and remember to alternate the fingers. With the left hand leave the fingers on where possible. For instance, when playing the progression F, G, F, the F should remain placed when you play the G. It is then ready when you want to play the F again.

COUNTING

Count the beats as you play, either out loud or in your head. It is the only sure way of measuring the time for each note, and if you form this habit at the very beginning you will progress much faster. Some people find that tapping the right foot helps to keep the beat even. The first beat of each measure should have a slight extra stress as it is the important downbeat (the conductor's baton always comes *down* on the first beat). Remember that you can go as slowly as you like as long as you give each note its proper time value.

Exercise 1

With this and all later exercises you are only concerned with the upper staff. The lower one is for the teacher.

The numbers beside the notes indicate left-hand fingering, *not the frets*, although they often coincide.

You will learn the notes more quickly if you do *not* write the letters (E, F, G, etc.) underneath them.

Exercise 2

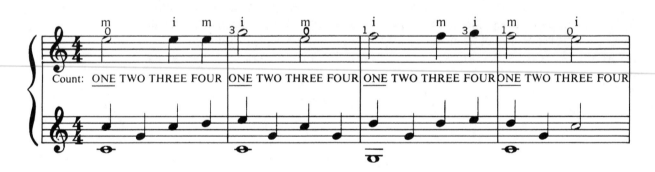

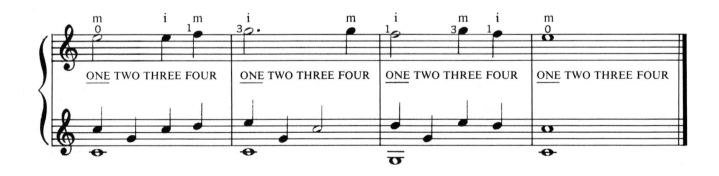

Exercise 3

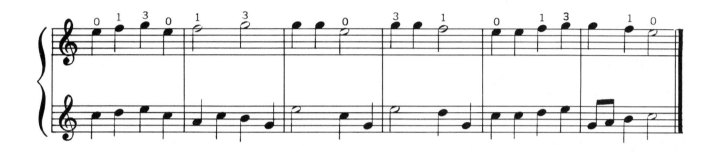

Exercise 4

In this exercise the left-hand fingering has been omitted to ensure that you read from the notes rather than the numbers. Remember to keep up the alternation.

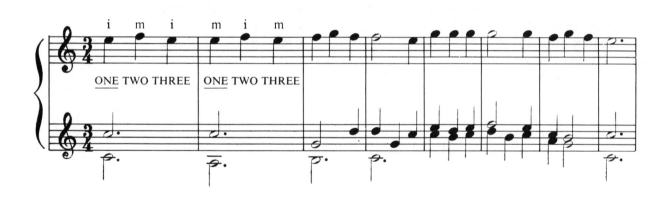

NOTES ON THE SECOND STRING

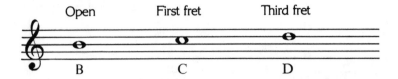

Open	First fret	Third fret
B	C	D

𝄽 = Quarter note rest

▬ = Half note rest

▬ = Whole note rest

RESTS AND DAMPING

Since a rest sign calls for a period of silence, it is necessary to be able to stop a string from sounding when a rest occurs.

With a stopped string (i.e. when a left-hand finger is used) all that is necessary is to release the pressure of the left hand finger from the fingerboard. The finger can still be in contact with the string; it is not necessary to take it off completely.

With an open string an easy way to damp the sound is to touch the string with the pad of the finger that would play next. For example, if you have just played the open first string with *i,* touch it with the pad of *m* to stop the sound. This may sound complicated, but is in fact very easy when you have done it a few times.

Exercise 5

In measure five, notice that the *i* finger is repeated. This is done sometimes after a long note or a rest, in cases when "changing step" results in smoother fingering in the measures to come.

In measure nine the fourth finger of the left hand is used on the G; this makes the transition from G to D smoother than a jump of the third finger.

Exercise 6

Exercise 7

As before, the left-hand fingering is omitted to check your note recognition.

PICK-UP NOTES

Music does not always begin on the first beat of the measure. There are sometimes one or more notes which precede the first stressed downbeat, and these are known as "pick-up" notes. When a piece begins with an incomplete measure, the final measure will also be incomplete, and the two will add up to one full measure.

The counting is not difficult as long as you identify which beat of the measure you start on, and count it accordingly. The song that follows shows how to do this.

THE BANKS OF THE OHIO   Traditional

NOTES ON THE THIRD STRING

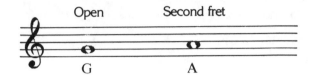

Open   Second fret

G   A

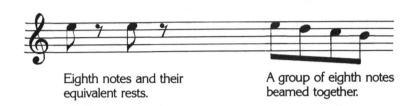

Eighth notes and their equivalent rests.

A group of eighth notes beamed together.

COUNTING EIGHTH NOTES

Eighth notes are twice as fast as quarter notes, so a way has to be found to divide the main counts in two. This is done by inserting the work "and" between the main counts.

Quarter Notes

ONE   TWO   THREE   FOUR

Eighth Notes

ONE and TWO and THREE and FOUR and

Notice that the number counts go at exactly the same speed in both examples, but the insertion of the "ands" in the second example gives the effect of doubling the time. Play and count the examples before going on to the exercises.

Exercise 8

Exercise 9

Exercise 10

This exercise is based on an extract from the song "Flow Gently Sweet Afton,"
music by James E. Spilman.

AURA LEE

George R. Poulton

NOTES ON THE FOURTH STRING

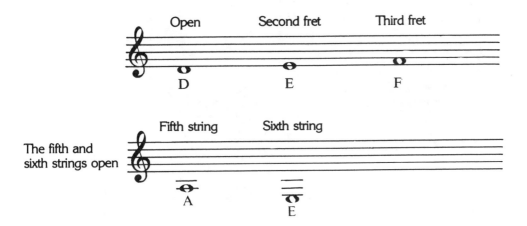

THUMB TECHNIQUE

The lower three strings are usually played with the thumb. The thumb may play a rest or a free stroke, the free stroke being by far the most common. The reason for this is that the lower strings tend to have greater natural resonance and therefore respond sufficiently to the lighter free stroke. In addition in a fast passage with the thumb; it is easier to repeat free strokes than rest strokes.

The thumb rest stroke does have its place, but this is usually reserved for passages of particular emphasis.

The illustrations demonstrate the two strokes, which should be tried experimentally before proceeding to the exercises.

Play Exercises 11 and 12, first with the free stroke, then for completeness try them with the rest stroke as well.

THUMB TECHNIQUE

Fig. 10 THE THUMB.

A. Like the fingernail the thumbnail is filed to an even curve.

C. Preparation. The string is in contact with the pad of the thumb, close to, but not touching the nail.

B. The angle of the thumb as it prepares to play.

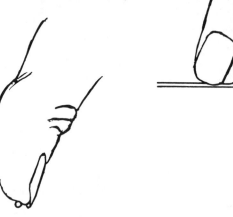

D. Completion, rest stroke. The thumb comes to rest against the next string.

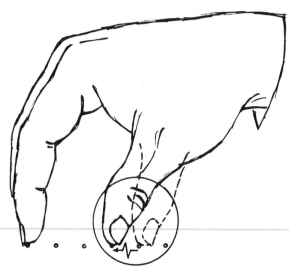

E. Completion, the free stroke. The thumb sweeps clear of the adjacent string.

F. This joint does not bend while doing either stroke.

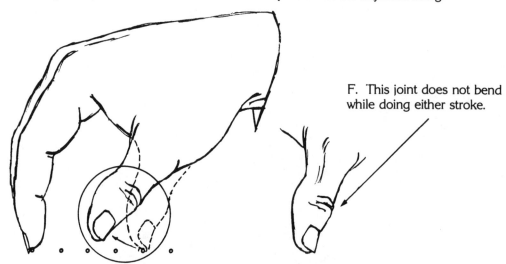

Exercise 11

Use the thumb throughout.

Exercise 12

Notice the use of the letter *p* to indicate the thumb, derived from the Spanish word "pulgar."

Exercise 13

This exercise is based on a famous chorale theme, for which J. S. Bach did many settings. In moving from thumb to fingers, try to avoid moving the hand. First use free strokes with the thumb, rest strokes with the fingers.

After you have played the piece a few times, try using free strokes with the fingers on all third-string notes, and rest strokes on the second and first strings. Although a little complicated to remember, this fingering will feel more natural.

NOTES ON THE FIFTH AND SIXTH STRINGS

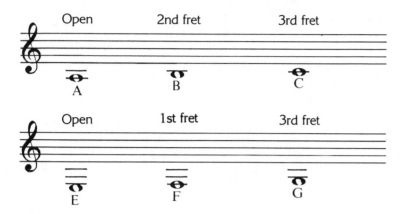

The notes below the staff are harder to memorize for some students, so the following exercises should be studied carefully and repeated where necessary. Distinguish particularly between the A on the *second* ledger line and the F on the *third*. In the same way be careful not to confuse the low E with the G since at first they look somewhat similar.

As soon as you are really familiar with these lower notes the way will be open to playing chords, arpeggios, and more complex pieces.

Exercise 14
In measure eleven notice that the fourth finger is used on the C, instead of the more usual third finger. This is to avoid jumping the third finger from string to string.

FANDANGO   Traditional

Exercise 15

The bass notes have been left unfingered so that you may check how well
you know them.

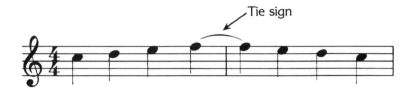

Ties

When two notes are joined by a TIE SIGN only the first is played, but it is held for the time value of both notes. This is particularly useful when a note is required to last from one measure to another.

In the example the F is held for two beats. The correct count for the two measures would be: "One Two Three *Four One* Two Three Four."

Exercise 16

SHARPS AND FLATS

Sharps (♯) and Flats (♭) are known as *accidentals* when they appear in the course of a piece. A sharp *raises* a note by a half step (one fret). A flat *lowers* a note by a half step.

Examples

A flat note a half step below an open string must be found on the next lower string. This will normally be at the fourth fret of the lower string.

Examples

The exception is the B flat, which is found at the *third* fret of the third string. You will remember from your tuning that the distance from the second to the third stirng is different from the others.

Example

34

A sharp or flat sign affects not only the note beside which it is placed, but all other occurrences of the same note for the remainder of the measure. Thus if an F is sharped at the beginning of a measure, all F's that follow in the same measure must also be sharped.

Example

both F's
are sharped.

This can be cancelled, however, by the use of a *Natural* sign (♮).

Example

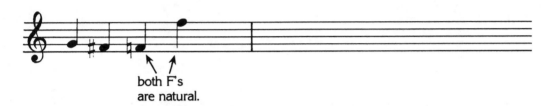

both F's
are natural.

Play the example below several times until you fully understand the effects of the various accidentals.

Example

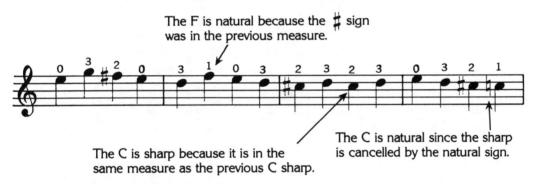

The F is natural because the ♯ sign
was in the previous measure.

The C is sharp because it is in the
same measure as the previous C sharp.

The C is natural since the sharp
is cancelled by the natural sign.

Exercise 17

Exercise 18

MINUET

Henry Purcell

CHORD TECHNIQUE

Two or more notes played simultaneously are known as a chord. The technique used for chords is that of the free stroke for both fingers and thumb.

The illustration below shows a simple chord played by *i* and *m* on the top two strings. At the end of the movement both fingers are clear of the adjacent strings.

Fig. 11 A TWO-NOTE CHORD PLAYED BY *I* AND *M*.

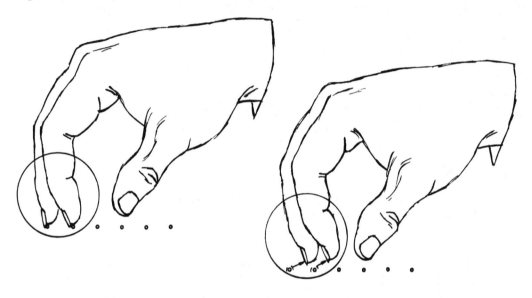

In Figure 12 the chord is played by the thumb and middle finger. At the completion of the movement, both thumb and fingers will be above the strings, but the *hand does not pull out from the strings*. The movement may be compared to an aircraft partially retracting its undercarriage without itself gaining height.

Whether there are two, three, or four notes in a chord, the technique is essentially the same. The important thing to remember is that the fingers should be placed in position on the strings before playing — do not snatch at the chord.

Fig. 12 A CHORD PLAYED BY *P* AND *M*.

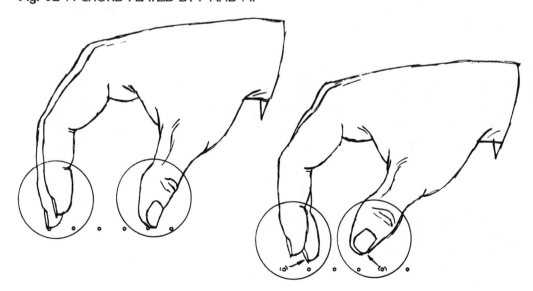

Exercise 19

This chord study introduces the use of the ring (a) finger, which becomes increasingly important as you progress with chords and arpeggios. Follow the right-hand fingering exactly, since it is comfortable and natural to the hand.

Exercise 20

Based on the popular Spanish theme "La Folia," this exercise starts simply but is progressive in difficulty. Remember not to lift the hand when playing the chords.

THE CHERRY SONG   Traditional

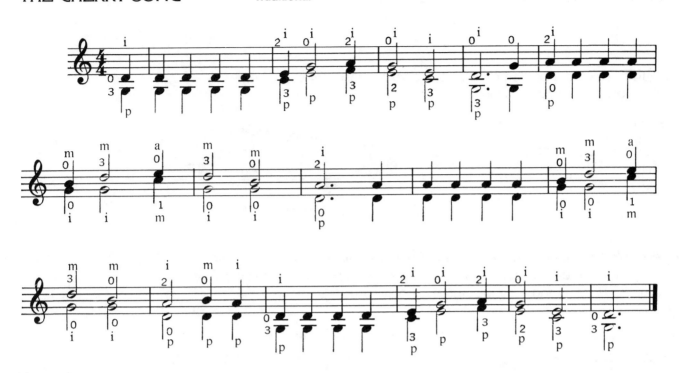

Exercise 21

All the chords may be played with *p, i* and *m.* Notice that although it may take longer to learn the notes at first the three note chords are not significantly more difficult to play.

ARPEGGIOS AND TRIPLETS

An ARPEGGIO is a broken chord, i.e. a chord whose notes are played in succession instead of simultaneously.

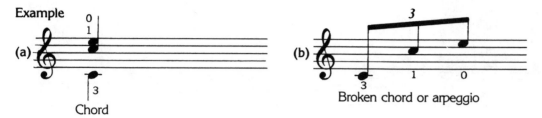

In example (b) the 3 above the group of notes shows that the three notes occupy the time of one quarter note. The group is known as a TRIPLET, and is counted "One - and - a" with three even syllables.

Example

Count: One and a Two and a Three and a Four and a

In a succession of triplets. as above, the three is often only indicated over the first group.

TECHNIQUE OF THE ARPEGGIO

The technique for playing arpeggios differs according to the direction of the notes played by the fingers. In the explanation below the two types of arpeggio are distinguished as "upward" or "downward" as shown in these examples.

Example

THE UPWARD ARPEGGIO
The direction of the notes played by
i and *m* is upward in pitch.

THE DOWNWARD ARPEGGIO
The pattern played by *m* and *i*
descends in pitch.

42

The Upward Arpeggio

This very common form of arpeggio starts with the selection of all the notes as if to play a chord. Then each finger plays a free stroke as shown in the illustrations.

Fig. 13 THE UPWARD ARPEGGIO.

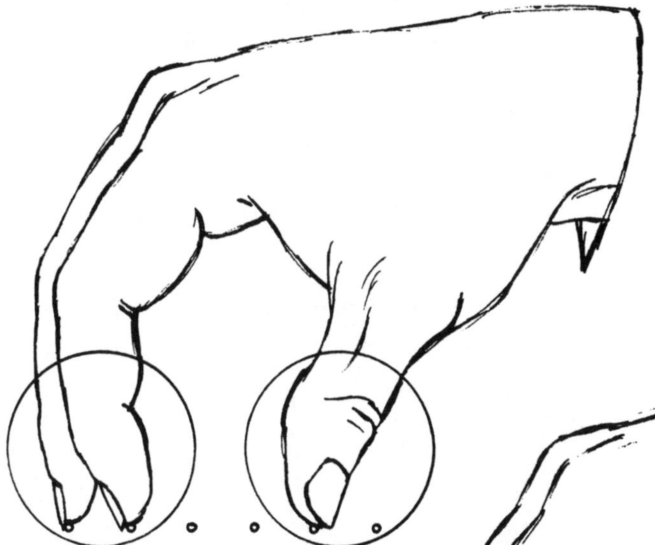

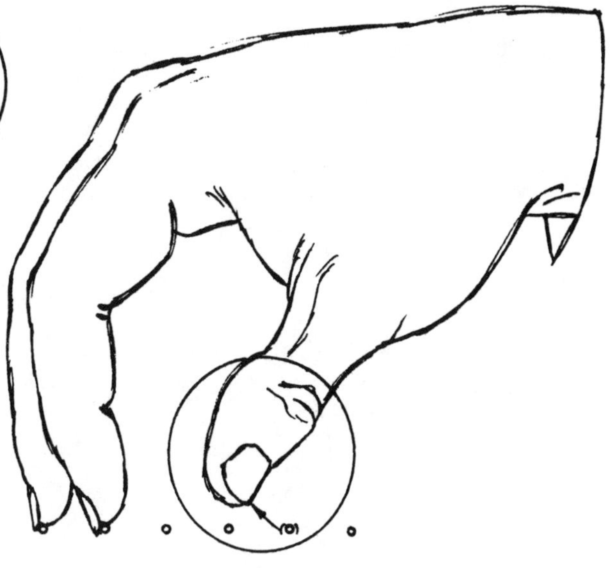

B. The thumb plays leaving the two fingers in position.

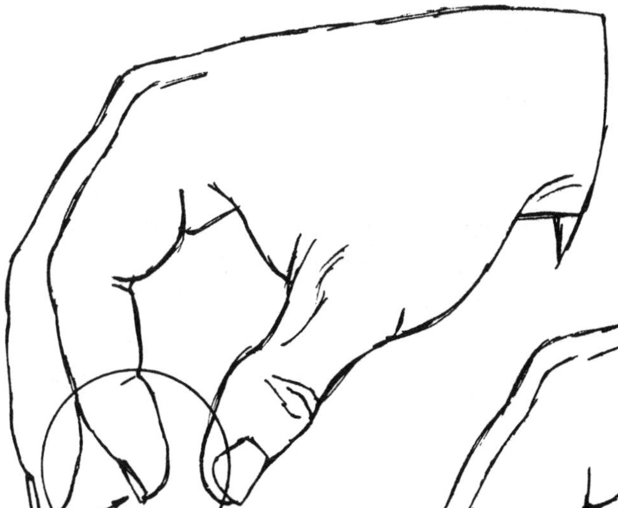

A. The fingers are prepared as if to play a chord.

D. The *m* finger plays completing the movement.

C. The *i* finger plays a free stroke.

The Downward Arpeggio

For the downward arpeggio *only the thumb and the finger on the highest string* are prepared in advance. Then the fingers play in succession as illustrated below.

Fig. 14 THE DOWNWARD ARPEGGIO.

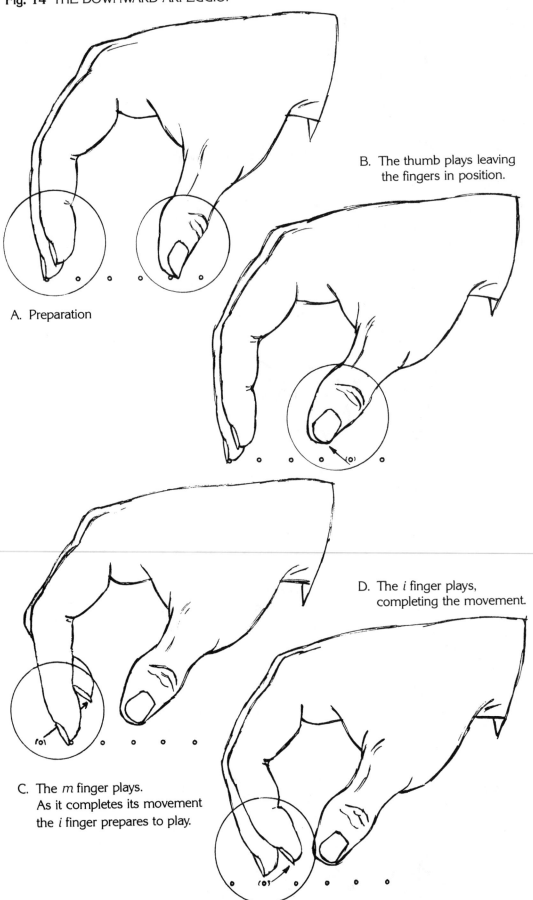

A. Preparation

B. The thumb plays leaving the fingers in position.

C. The *m* finger plays. As it completes its movement the *i* finger prepares to play.

D. The *i* finger plays, completing the movement.

Exercise 22

Play the chords first to learn the left-hand pattern, then practice the upward arpeggio.

Exercise 23

In this exercise the *m* finger should be in position before the thumb plays in each triplet group.

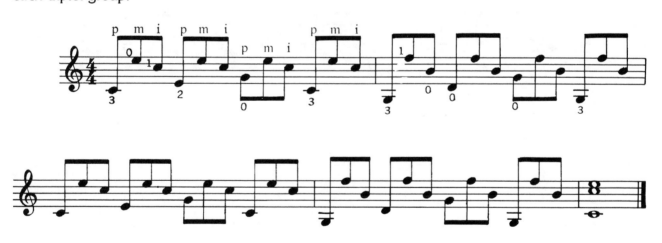

Exercise 24

Based on the study in three-note chords, this exercise may be used to practice the downward arpeggio as well.

COMBINING CHORDS AND MELODY

The main techniques for melody, chord, and arpeggio have now been learned; and the next step involves combining these techniques so that you will be able to play more interesting solos.

Melody and chords may be simply combined by holding one note of a chord while the other note is varied to form a melody.

Example

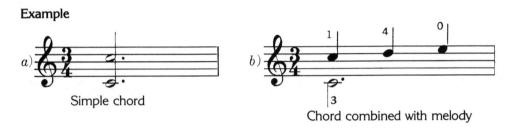

a) Simple chord

b) Chord combined with melody

In (b) above the third finger remains on the low C so that it will continue to sound while the upper C, D and E are played.

Exercise 25

In this exercise the right-hand fingering shows that when chords and melody are mixed the alternation is not strict and fingers are occasionally repeated. Try to see from the music why this is done.

Use free strokes throughout.

Exercise 26

Use free strokes throughout

Sometimes the upper part of the chord is held while the lower part moves. The parts are often referred to as VOICES, since each may be compared to an individual singer.

In the example it would be usual to say that the movement is in the lower, or bass, voice.

The two voices do not necessarily start on the same beat, and often move quite independently.

Example

As complicated as this may look at first, it can be quite easily "solved" by considering what happens on each beat. Here is the procedure for playing the first measure:

First Beat   Play the low C to start the lower voice.

Second Beat   Play the high C to start the upper voice. The low C must continue sounding.

Third Beat   Play the upper voice E. The third finger is *still* on the low C so that it continues to sound.

The second measure proceeds as follows:

First Beat   Play the upper voice D

Second Beat   Play the open-string G. The fourth finger *remains on the high D* so that it continues to sound.

Third Beat   Play the F on the fourth string. The little finger is *still* holding down the D.

Work through the above steps until the procedure is quite clear. You will notice that there is no particular difficulty in reading music in two lines: The secret is to decide what happens on each beat.

LA VOLTA

16th-Century Dance

The repeat sign ![repeat sign] indicates that the first eight measures are played twice.

PRACTICE SUGGESTIONS

The pieces that follow have been chosen to enable you to practice all that you have learned so far, and to provide a beginning repertory of enjoyable music. They should be thoroughly studied before moving on to Part Two, and to ensure the best results the following suggestions are offered for practicing.

1. At this stage several short practice periods during the day will produce much better results than a single longer period.

2. Always take a break after about fifteen minutes of intensive practice. Your ability to learn is far greater after a pause for relaxation.

3. Do not attempt to practice when you are tired or not in the mood. You may feel virtuous, but the time is wasted.

4. Be patient with yourself and go slowly. This way the speed will come naturally in due course, and you will avoid the frustration that comes from trying to run before you can walk.

5. Keep in mind that the purpose is to make beautiful sounds, and that this can be done at an early stage and with very simple music.

6. At some time you will feel that your progress has been halted, and that you are on a plateau. This feeling is shared by almost everyone, and if you realize this and continue your regular practicing without feeling incompetent or discouraged you will soon pass through the stage and on to further achievement.

7. Realize that the difficulties you encounter are shared by most students. As one example, the chord which looks so simple on paper is very difficult for almost all beginners. However, with practice the awkwardness disappears, and in time you will forget that it was ever a problem.

8. Enjoy yourself. Whatever your long-term goal may be the day to day practice can, and should, be a source of pleasure and satisfaction.

MOORISH DANCE

Traditional

EVENING BREEZE

F.M. Noad

ETUDE

Ferdinando Carulli (1770-1841)

In this piece the indication "Da Capo" means repeat from the beginning, "al fine" means "to the place marked *fine* or end." When playing Da Capo the other repeats are ignored.

MINUET THEME

Wolfgang Amadeus Mozart (1756-1791)

FLAMENCO STUDY

Traditional

SONG AT NIGHTFALL

C.M. Bellman